Facts About the Humpback Whale

By Lisa Strattin

© 2019 Lisa Strattin

FREE BOOK

FREE FOR ALL SUBSCRIBERS

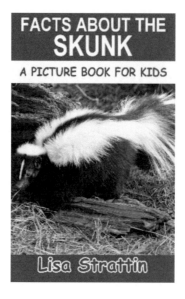

LisaStrattin.com/Subscribe-Here

BOX SET

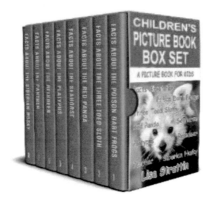

- FACTS ABOUT THE POISON DART FROGS
- FACTS ABOUT THE THREE TOED SLOTH
- FACTS ABOUT THE RED PANDA
- FACTS ABOUT THE SEAHORSE
- FACTS ABOUT THE PLATYPUS
- FACTS ABOUT THE REINDEER
- FACTS ABOUT THE PANTHER
- FACTS ABOUT THE SIBERIAN HUSKY

LisaStrattin.com/BookBundle

Facts for Kids Picture Books by Lisa Strattin

Little Blue Penguin, Vol 92

Chipmunk, Vol 5

Frilled Lizard, Vol 39

Blue and Gold Macaw, Vol 13

Poison Dart Frogs, Vol 50

Blue Tarantula, Vol 115

African Elephants, Vol 8

Amur Leopard, Vol 89

Sabre Tooth Tiger, Vol 167

Baboon, Vol 174

Sign Up for New Release Emails Here

LisaStrattin.com/subscribe-here

Contents

INTRODUCTION

The Humpback Whale is one of the larger species of whale in the ocean today. They are seen and photographed by many people who go on a "whale sightseeing tour" during the time of the year that they are migrating.

CHARACTERISTICS

The Humpback Whales spend the summer months in the colder, polar waters and then they migrate south in the winter to the warmer waters where they live off of their fat reserves until they migrate north again in the summer. The average humpback whale can travel to around 15,000 miles every year migrating.

They have not one, but two, blow holes located on the top of their head. These allow the whale to breathe in air when they are on the surface of the water. They spout (breathe) around 1-2 times per minute when resting, and 4-8 times per minutes after they make a deep dive into the ocean.

The blow (spout of water that appears) of this whale is a double stream of spray that rises as much as 13 feet into the air above the surface of the water.

APPEARANCE

The Humpback Whale is a species of Baleen Whale and they are thought to be closely related to the Blue Whale and the Minke Whale. This means that the Humpback Whale has rows of plates in their huge mouth, which the whale uses to filter small particles of food out of the water. They do not have teeth, so they eat by filtering these particles and swallowing them.

REPRODUCTION

Humpback Whale mothers usually give birth to their young during the winter months when in the warmer, southern waters. The mother feeds her calf on the milk that she produces. This means that the mother is sometimes very weak when returning to the colder, northern waters because she might not have eaten since the migration to the warmer water began months before.

LIFE SPAN

Humpback Whales live for 50 to 60 years!

SIZE

An adult Humpback Whale can grow to be as long as 52 feet and weigh between 40 and 100 tons!

They are HUGE!

HABITAT

Humpback Whales are found in all of the main oceans worldwide, but they tend to stay in three main herds, the Atlantic, the Pacific and the Indian Ocean herds.

DIET

Humpback Whales primarily feed off krill and plankton that are abundantly present in richer waters. They will also eat small fish and crabs that get pulled into their mouth while filtering large amounts of water.

ENEMIES

The only known marine animal that is known to hunt the Humpback Whale is the Killer Whale.

SUITABILITY AS PETS

Well, of course the Humpback Whale is not a marine animal you could keep as a pet. But if you want to see one of these beautiful creatures, you might see them if you go on a whale sightseeing tour sometime. They are too big even for most aquariums to have them, but you can see many pictures of them and even some documentaries that tell you all about them.

COLOR ME

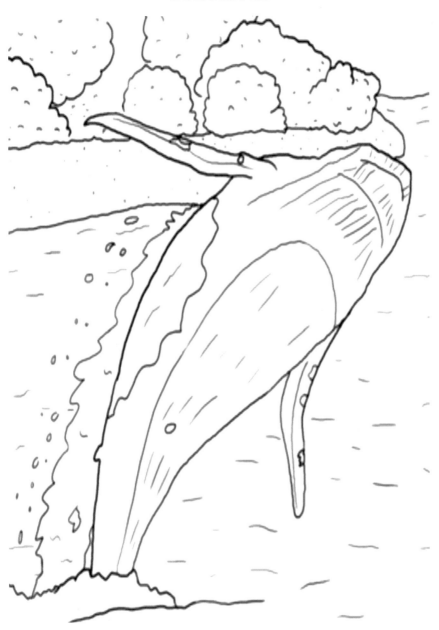

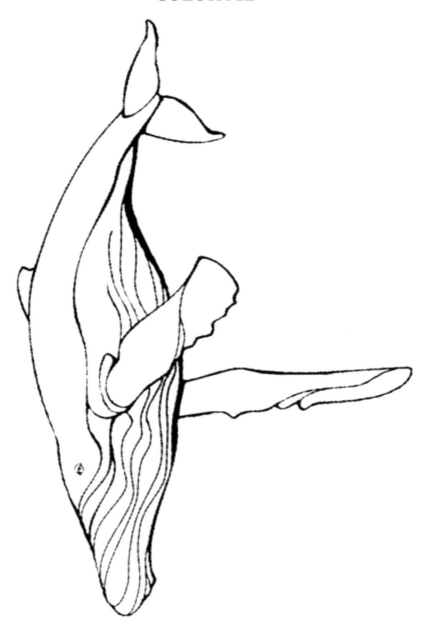

COLOR ME

COLOR ME

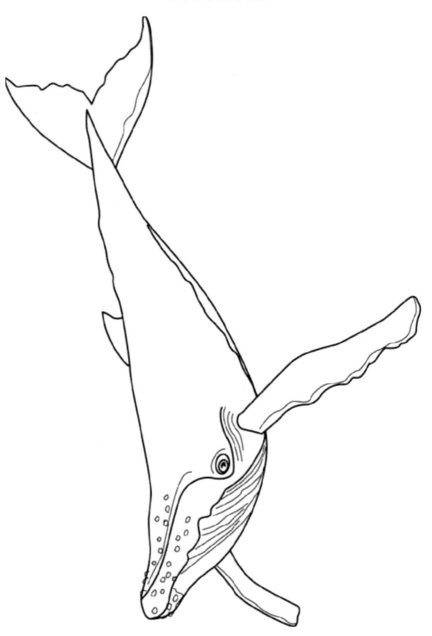

Please leave me a review here:

LisaStrattin.com/Review-Vol-294

For more Kindle Downloads Visit Lisa Strattin
Author Page on Amazon Author Central

amazon.com/author/lisastrattin

To see upcoming titles, visit my website at
LisaStrattin.com– most books available on Kindle!

LisaStrattin.com

FREE BOOK

FOR ALL SUBSCRIBERS – SIGN UP NOW

LisaStrattin.com/Subscribe-Here

LisaStrattin.com/Facebook

LisaStrattin.com/Youtube

Made in United States
Troutdale, OR
12/17/2023

16069680R00026